Little Red H

Story written by Karra McFarlane
Illustrated by Tim Archbold

Speed Sounds

Consonants   *Ask children to say the sounds.*

f ff ph	l ll (le)	m mm mb	n nn kn gn	r rr wr	s ss se c ce	v ve	z zz se s	sh	th	ng nk

b (bb)	c k ck	d dd	g gg gu	h	j g ge dge	p pp	qu	t tt	w wh	x	y	ch (tch)

Each box contains one sound but sometimes more than one grapheme.
*Focus graphemes for this story are **circled**.*

Vowels

Ask children to say the sounds in and out of order.

a	e ea	i	o	u	ay	ee y	igh i	ow o
at	hen	in	on	up	day	see	high	blow

oo	oo	(ar)	or oor ore	air	ir	ou	oy oi
zoo	look	car	for	fair	whirl	shout	boy

5

Story Green Words

cart   crops   mill   flour*   eat*   ground*

Ask children to say the syllables and then read the whole word.

farm|yard   self|ish   litt|le   hea|vy

Ask children to read the root first and then the whole word with the suffix.

seed → seeds   greed → greedy   ask → asked

harvest → harvested   peck → pecking   snooze → snoozing

bark → barked   crush → crushed

* Challenge Words

6

Vocabulary Check

Discuss the meaning (as used in the story) after the children have read each word.

	definition:	sentence:
screeched	cried in a loud, high voice	"Not I," screeched the selfish cat.
tended	looked after	Little Red Hen tended the crops day by day.
crops	plants that farmers grow as food	The crops got big and tall.
harvest	picking crops when they're grown	"Who will help me to harvest the crops?"
mill	the place where the crops are made into flour	"Who will help me to push the cart up the hill to the mill?"
snoozing	sleeping in the daytime	Then, Little Red Hen spotted Dog snoozing next to a tree.
gobbling	eating quickly	She spotted Duck in the pond, gobbling up all the weeds.

Red Words

Ask children to practise reading the words across the rows, down the columns and in and out of order clearly and quickly.

there	watch	tall	some
other	over	some	one
were	who	she	her
one	all	said	are
my	do	by	where

Little Red Hen

Little Red Hen lived on a farm with a sleepy dog, a greedy duck and a selfish cat.

One day she was pecking in the farmyard when she spotted lots of seeds on the ground.

"Who will help me to plant the seeds on the farm?"
Little Red Hen asked the other animals.

"Not I," barked the sleepy dog.

"Not I," quacked the greedy duck.

"Not I," screeched the selfish cat.

So Little Red Hen planted the seeds, all by herself.

Little Red Hen tended the crops day by day. The crops got big and tall.

"Who will help me to harvest the crops?" asked Little Red Hen.
"Not I," barked the sleepy dog.
"Not I," quacked the greedy duck.
"Not I," screeched the selfish cat.

So Little Red Hen harvested the crops until it was dark, all by herself.

Little Red Hen lifted all the crops she had harvested into a cart.

"Who will help me to push the cart up the hill to the mill?" asked Little Red Hen.

She looked all over the farmyard, but the sleepy dog, the greedy duck and the selfish cat were nowhere to be seen.

Then, Little Red Hen spotted Dog snoozing next to a tree.
She spotted Duck in the pond, gobbling up all the weeds.
She spotted Cat playing with a robin.

So Little Red Hen took the crops up the hill to the mill, all by herself.

At the mill, Little Red Hen crushed the crops
into flour, all by herself. She took the heavy
sack of flour back to the farm, all by herself.

In the kitchen, Little Red Hen
mixed the flour and cooked
the bread in a tin, all
by herself.

Then Little Red Hen took the fresh, crusty bread
into the farmyard...

"That looks good!" barked the sleepy dog.
"What a good cook you are!" quacked the greedy duck.
"You have a lot of bread there!" screeched the selfish cat.
"Yes, I do," said Little Red Hen. "Let's eat the bread,
my little chicks," she clucked.

Dog, Duck and Cat watched as the chicks pecked at the bread.
"May we have some too?" they asked.

What do you think Little Red Hen said?

Questions to talk about

Ask children to TTYP each question using 'Fastest finger' (FF) or 'Have a think' (HaT).

p.9 (FF)   Who lives on the farm with Little Red Hen?

p.10 (HaT) When little Red Hen asked the animals to help her, they said 'Not I'. Why didn't they help?

p.12 (FF)   Little Red Hen needed help after harvesting. What help did she need?

p.13 (HaT) Why does Little Red Hen take the crops to the mill herself?

p.14 (HaT) Little Red Hen didn't ask for any help to bake the bread. Why?

p.15 (HaT) What did the animals think when the chicks ate the bread?

p.15 (HaT) The story doesn't tell us what Little Red Hen said at the end. What do you think she said?

Questions to read and answer

(Children complete without your help.)

1. Dog, Duck and Cat said **"yes / maybe / not I"** when Little Red Hen asked them to help.

2. Dog was **selfish / sleepy / greedy**.

3. Cat was playing with **a robin / the crops / some seeds**.

4. Little Red Hen took the crops to the **farm / mill / barn**.

5. Little Red Hen let the **cat / dog / chicks** eat the fresh bread.

Speedy Green Words

Ask children to practise reading the words across the rows, down the columns and in and out of order clearly and quickly.

playing	fresh	may	bread
next	carry	dark	good
tree	greedy	farm	too
day	may	plant	next
cooked	seen	heavy	look